A Piece of Peace

Gene Berd

BookLeaf
Publishing

India | USA | UK

Presentation by *BookLeaf Publishing*

Web: www.bookleafpub.com

E-mail: info@bookleafpub.com

ISBN: 9789357612197

First edition 2022

ACKNOWLEDGE MENT

I am grateful for all the lessons, difficult and easy, that life has taught me. I am so grateful to my parents, and the many aunts and uncles that raised me. The many, many teachers of life I have met on my journey, the young and the old. I am so amazed and joyful for your participation in my life, even if only for a tiny moment. Thank you all.
Lastly, a huge thank you, and "I love you" to my many siblings. Your listening ears have offered me so many lessons. I love you.

PREFACE

Take a moment, take a breath and enjoy any
piece or collection of pieces.
What peace you find, is yours.
It feels wonderful to know that you may gain a
little ease in your life through this.

Dear reader,

Please take some time and illustrate on these
empty pages. This book is yours, all yours. I
would enjoy knowing that you took the liberty
of drawing all over it and would LOVE to see
any illustrations you make posted up on the
internet.
Please tag me @berdbooks or #pieceofpeace
when you post these illustrations, so that I can
see them!

With compassionate love
Gene Berd.

Hugs and Love

A homeless winter
Nightly bar crawl with hand-washed glassware.
Morning stretch with the day-care mommies.

Tied my bike to street West 34.
Walked the stairs, Korean door.
Changed my shirt, served a drink.
The d train home, usual stink.

Wriggle your fingers, my friends!
Would you play a game with me?
How many fingers do you see?

Brand new people, with no clue
make my day and it is true:
I learned to love from my 5-year-old friends.

One hug at a time I understood that the world is
changed one hug at a time. One smile at a time.
One heart at a time. Love

I spent the next years searching and sure have
found it.

The center to my Tootsie Pop, I found it on hug three hundred and fifty-two.
Just short a few days from New year's Eve I found that love is made of friendship. No, not convincingly contrived convenience, but ships you build with friends to carry love.

Some ships will sink and some will breach, but with love and effort on this day and on this beach, anything is possible in a friendship.

So say hello and start to build your mast, your hull.

Hullo.

Nature is Wild

Nature is wild.

Nature is love.

Nature is flow.
Nature is blood.
Nature is fire.
Nature will rip your heart out and eat it in front
of you.
Decompose.
Recompose.
Build anew.
Renew.

Nature is love.

Nature is wild.

Water your Cactus

My name's sake once said "don't forget to water
your cactus"
The next day he was no more.
I don't forget those words; they mean more and
more as time goes on
Within every situation I run those words, my
mind connects new meanings
I think he meant my mother
I think he meant myself
I think he meant to make sure I wet my stick
I'm sure he meant to water the plants
As I grow older all those meetings fall away
He said to water the cactus and I heard
Love yourself and those around you.

Howl.0

Breathless howl of lovers past.
I miss you so.
You
Your breath
Your rising-falling chest.
And yet
I feel at peace without your rhythm.
It took too many years for me to gain
Control of my own breath.
To count to 4 and 4 again until
One time you no longer entered
My mind
Became a clear oasis
Present moment
Now...
And
Now, again.
I gained and regained composure.
Until I built my posture and exposed
My faults and failures to myself
Forgave them all and gave myself
To me
To me, I called my angels, my powers, and my
God.
I asked for mercy, strength and love.

I received in troves
All that I had begged for from you, from me.

Tend your Garden

Tend your garden well.
It feeds the fruits of your labors, waters the trees
of your thoughts, and washes your worries.

Tend your garden well.
The fruits need constant picking and the
channels need cleaning.
Pick your battles judiciously, for they will build
your battleground and you will either eat of your
garden or be eaten by it.

Tend your garden well.
Observe the flow of life upon your garden.
There are creatures lurking who will waste your
waters, prune your fruits and foul your fowl.
Pluck those who do not tend your garden well.
Especially if they are you.

Tend your garden well.
Give love and gratitude for the soil, the rain and
sun that giveth. They may taketh any day.

Intimacy

I Speak to the bits of you that reside in my
wound that you tried to heal.
Committed to a person and relationship,unable
to speak.
Unable to reach those bits and share perspectives
for a moment.
Unwilling to shift perspectives, even for a
minute.
Do these pieces live forever?
Is there a setting on this pain I can turn off?
Like WiFi, Always transmitting.

In to me, I see.

Unity

A gift, expecting nothing in return.
You surrendered a part of your energy to my
agenda.

I speak to the bits of me that reside in your
wound, that I tried to heal.

Felt, not seen, nor heard.
Palpable, measured, and substantive.
Every bond is different.

Separated by the 4th dimension.
I call to those pieces, but the cord is cut
no one is on the other line.

The nature of unity.
It is me and me.

Watermelon is for Sharing

Watermelon is for sharing
In times of need, take heed.
The ones around you are just the same.
Eating, drinking, sleeping, ...

You buy a melon full of water.
The sun-warmed sugars dripping out the cracks.
Take a slice, take a bite and invite your neighbor
Pikey.

This is watermelon, there is no race,
there is no gender, put it in a blender
and suck the juices off the table.

Free of Liberation

I feel bad for Loud
He gets all the Flack
Silent never hears a peep
He gets all the time to sleep.

Lets begin

It is beauty that killed the beast.
Lets begin. She lay on water, Fresh.Simple.
Begin. One word　　　　Frozen.
at　A　time.
One line at　a　time.
One　smile.
At　a　time.

Place Coffee Stain Here

Coffee stain, oh coffee stain, how I wonder
about your meanings.
Dragons, women, mountains, all have appeared
before me here.
Eagle headed giant on a throne of spirit totem,
Flowing from the source tree. The singularity.
Good morning.
Isn't it?

Empty not-book

Empty not-book
Filllll e d r i g h t u p.
Word by word
		Material materialized
		Symbol and sign
For myself to see for my inner-me.
My victory.
		Little by little the words you see
Spelled,
My victory.
With love
Always and in all ways.
Gene

I just is

Let it be.
Just be
I am.

                (some times it is hard to
do)

              There is no practice,
just be.

        You just are. Just observe. Be.

       Fully autonomous devoid of self, devoid
of being
Playing time.
Breathing through it all.

              Doubting my validity,
        It's a healthy check on ego
      still, it is still apiece of ego.
Wishing to share, help or participate
It too is a piece of ego
The untapped mind
Open and shut, all in between
Here and now.o0o..
I don't mind
I, is i , I just is.
I

Smiling by the fire, we are enough.

Together, by the fire
Pleiades shining, Jupiter smiling
Spitting fire lines
Spinning fire rhymes
Soul-sisters, soul-brothers, soul tribe.
One reflected in all, all enfolded in one.
Cosmic mirrors present in flesh,
Journeys and crossroads presenting fresh.
Holding space to initiate transformations
Healing beings transmuting for the selves within
ourselves,
for one another, for ourselves.

Idiocracy call

We all heard the over-population call
It said there were too many of us all.
And now we wrapped our willies,
Tied our tubes and celibately held our sillies.

Thus we birthed the Brave New World
Betas, gammas, epsilons & deltas, we sold our
Intelligence, for gold-plated apples, watches,
razors.
And so the Alpha Double Plus would kindly
remember us
We sold our reproductive rights to do "what's
right."

Cosmic Communication

Sex and love are
Communications too.
They're meant to exist b/w
At least the two
Polarities would help And boundaries may help
too
Speaker & listener do the double duty,
Listening and speaking; gyrating, cosmic beauty.

Dangers of poor Self-care

You've forgot that you're a cactus.
You need water sun and air.
You need grit & struggle to survive.
You need rest and baths and sweat and tears
But mostly you need self-love and a little love
Of your peers.

Begin again

Begin again. Gather yourself. Find yourself next to your reflection.
Take a moment.
Take it.
Accept it all. Whatever you see, you are, you.
All of you that you see before you exists now.
There is more of you than you can see. Accept all of you. That is all. Smell, hear, taste, see, feel yourself. Know yourself. Intuit yourself. Sense yourself. Observe yourself. Entice yourself. Invoice yourself. Pay yourself. Expense yourself. Love yourself. Teach yourself. Experience yourself. Bless yourself. Manifest yourself. Consult yourself. Plan yourself. Shape yourself. Design yourself. Attend yourself. Sanctify yourself. Honor yourself. Celebrate yourself. Feed yourself. Tend yourself. Groom yourself. Strengthen yourself. Observe yourself. Engage yourself. Consume yourself. Order yourself. Command yourself. Relax yourself. Forgive yourself. Liberate yourself.
Become who you are. Who will be you is here.
Breathe.
Breathe. . . it is ok. Everything is ok. Really.
Breathe.

You are here. You can handle it. You got this.
You got it.
Breathe. It's ok. No, really. Take a moment.
Breathe,
 and
Begin again...

www.ingramcontent.com/pod-product-compliance
Lightning Source LLC
LaVergne TN
LVHW021356200726

843509LV00014B/2885